DIABETES

A Comprehensive Guide to
Diabetes in Cats

WRITTEN BY VETERINARY EXPERT

DR. GORDON ROBERTS BVSC MRCVS

Hello! My name is Gordon Roberts and I'm the author of this book. I hope you enjoy all of the specialist advice it contains. I'm a huge advocate of preventative care for animals, and I'd love to see more pet owners taking the time to research their pet's health care needs.

Being proactive and educating yourself about your pet's health now, rather than later on, could save you and your pet a lot of trouble in the long run.

If you'd like to read more of my professional pet care advice simply go to my website at http://drgordonroberts.com/freereportsdownload/.

As a thank you for purchasing this book, you'll find dozens of bonus pet care reports there to download and keep, absolutely free of charge!

Best wishes,

Gordon

Founder, Wellpets

Contents

Introduction

If your cat was recently diagnosed as diabetic, don't be disheartened. Around the world, thousands of cat owners like you are treating and managing their cat's diabetes successfully. Their cats are living normal, happy lives despite their diabetes, and yours can too.

This book will tell you the useful and important facts you need to know about diabetes including causes, symptoms, emergency signs to watch out for and frequently asked questions. In many cases, your vet will have explained things in brief, but it isn't always possible to take notes in such an unusual situation. Having the facts written down for you in plain English can be a huge help.

We've tried to avoid obscure veterinary and medical terms here, but if you do get stuck, simply turn to the back of the book where you'll find a useful glossary of diabetic terms. For those who are a little daunted at the prospect of becoming their cat's full time carer, there is a useful section on how to cope with the role of caregiver and how you can manage the condition effectively.

We hope you find the information here useful and easy to digest. Now is the time to be calmly gathering information, and you have taken the first step by buying this book. Your cat is going to thank you for it. We wish you both the best.

Chapter 1:
How diabetes occurs in cats

In order for you to really understand what's going on with your cat's health, you need to first get an understanding of how diabetes comes about. To help you truly grasp what diabetes means for your cat, here is a brief lesson in biology.

The pancreas

The main organ causing diabetes is the pancreas, which is a small pinkish organ in the folds of your cat's intestine. The pancreas has some important jobs to do, despite its small size. Firstly, it produces the enzymes necessary for your cat to digest her food. Secondly, it also produces some vital hormones, one of which is insulin. Insulin is secreted by the beta cells in the pancreas, which are located in an area called the Islets of Langerhans. Insulin is central to any discussion on diabetes, as you will soon learn. Cats with diabetes are usually not producing enough insulin, or their bodies are resistant to the insulin they are producing.

The role of insulin and glucose

Insulin regulates how your cat's body uses glucose. Glucose (or sugar) comes from the carbohydrates in your cat's food, and it is also sometimes produced by the liver. It is used as fuel for the body, and provides the energy source for some very important bodily functions.

How does insulin regulate glucose? Well, insulin is released into the blood stream where it gets to work on the glucose it finds there, allowing it to pass from the bloodstream into the millions of cells in the body. Brain cells, for example, need glucose in order to function properly and without it they can die off. So, insulin is really vital to making sure your cat's brain, and other organs, can carry out their normal jobs.

What does the body do without insulin?

If there is no insulin being produced by the pancreas, or if the insulin being produced simply stops being effective, the cat will develop what we call diabetes.

Here's what happens to your cat when diabetes occurs:

- The glucose floating around in the cat's bloodstream has no way to pass into the cells, where it is needed. So, more and more glucose builds up in the bloodstream (resulting in hyperglycemia or high blood sugar) and it is eventually filtered through the kidneys.
- The kidneys can only cope with so much sugar, and sooner or later (when they reach their "renal threshold") the excess glucose spills over into the cat's urine. This is the reason why so many diabetic cats suffer from excess urination – their bodies are trying as hard as they can to eliminate all the unused glucose.
- Without insulin and access to glucose, the cells are deprived of

their usual energy source and the body is forced to break down other substances, such as fat and muscle, instead.
- When the body breaks down too much fat, it floods the bloodstream with proteins called ketones, which can build up in toxic amounts and cause a condition called ketoacidosis.

All sorts of complications can arise if this situation is left untreated, which we'll go through later on in this book.

How is cat diabetes different to other forms of diabetes?

There are lots of similarities between diabetes in cats, and diabetes in dogs and humans. However, there are some subtle differences you should be aware of. When researching and treating diabetes, always make sure you get advice which relates specifically for cats.

The majority of cats (80-90%) develop diabetes that is similar to "type II" diabetes in humans. Here is a simple way to understand this:

Type II diabetes ("diabetes mellitus")

- The body either doesn't produce enough insulin, or produces insulin that isn't being absorbed properly by the cells (also known as insulin resistance).
- This is the most common form of diabetes for both cats and humans. It only happens rarely in dogs.

Type I diabetes

- The body stops producing insulin altogether. This usually happens as a result of the pancreas becoming chronically inflamed, which causes permanent damage to the beta cells that secrete insulin.
- The most common diabetes in dogs, though not very common in humans or cats.

It's more than likely that if your cat has diabetes it will start out as Type II, as mentioned above. Unfortunately, vets rarely know whether this diabetes happens because of a lack of insulin being produced by the pancreas, or because the insulin that the pancreas does produce is simply ineffective. The tests available to the veterinary world simply aren't as advanced as those found in human hospitals and clinics. What we do know, however, is that more and more cats are developing this Type II diabetes, which is significantly on the rise.

Important to know

Note that if your cat starts out having type II diabetes, and if they go untreated for a long time, the condition is very likely to progress into type I diabetes, where the cat becomes completely dependent on daily doses of insulin. This is just one of the many reasons why early diagnosis and treatment of diabetes is essential.

Chapter 2: What causes diabetes in cats?

Diabetes is a complex condition, and is usually caused by a combination of factors rather than one single culprit. Usually your vet won't be able to pinpoint an exact cause, but by going through the most common risk factors below, you should have a fair idea of what applies to your cat and what might have contributed to him developing the condition.

Male vs female cats

Diabetes is a lot more common in male cats than in female cats. If you have a male cat then you should be especially vigilant for the signs of diabetes, which we'll discuss later on. In particular, male cats that have been neutered are at the highest risk of developing this condition.

Genetics

Some breeds of cat are more prone to diabetes than others, so we know that there is a genetic link to the condition. The Burmese breed is particularly susceptible, for example. If you have a Burmese cat, or you're thinking of getting one, be sure to ask your breeder if there is a history of diabetes in the bloodline.

Age

Old age is certainly a risk factor that increases the likelihood of cats becoming diabetic. What's more, the symptoms of diabetes are quite similar to those of old age (weight loss, increased urination, lethargy). This makes it difficult for owners to recognise when their cats are genuinely ill. Because many owners confuse the signs of diabetes for those of old age, they delay going to the vet and the cat's health suffers more. If you have friends with older cats, it's a good idea to warn them about this all too common issue.

Obesity

There is a very strong link between obesity and diabetes in cats. Most cats that develop diabetes either are, or have been, overweight. Once your cat becomes obese, he is at a far greater risk of developing diabetes, so it's really important to keep an eye on his waistline, and his diet. Lots of cats that become obese are indoor cats, who don't get enough exercise and are fed too many treats by well-meaning owners. Don't be one of these people!

Take the time to think about what you feed your cat, and what his lifestyle is like. There are lots and lots of ways to make sure your cat keeps active, which we'll cover later on in this book. Once you get your cat's weight down, there is a good chance that his diabetes will improve too. The reasons why excess body fat has such an effect on diabetes is complex, but some research has shown that the fat cells themselves make insulin less effective in the body.

Pancreatitis

Many cats with diabetes turn out to have a chronic form of pancreatitis, where the pancreas becomes extremely inflamed over time. The inflamed pancreas leaks digestive enzymes which, instead of breaking down food in the gut, start to break down the areas of the pancreas which are responsible for producing insulin, destroying the beta cells.

This is a painful, serious condition. In cats, it can sometimes be part of a condition called triad disease, where instead of just a portion of the pancreas being affected, the entire pancreas and the surrounding organs become inflamed too. This is usually a result of excess stress on the organs caused by toxins in the cat's diet or environment. Some vets suspect that these toxins can come from the rancid ingredients in fish-based cat food products, which aren't nearly as fresh as the fish ingredients in human foods.

Poor diet

As we've discussed, obesity has a strong link to diabetes. So, it follows that diet is also a very common factor in developing the condition. Take a good look at what you're feeding your cat and the breakdown of ingredients on the label. Is it giving your cat the nutrients he needs? Or is it full of artificial ingredients, and unnecessary carbohydrates? Unfortunately, dry kibble is often full of starchy "filler" ingredients which fill your cat's bloodstream with excess sugars. In addition to this, a very fatty diet can put unnecessary strain on the liver and can lead to pancreatitis, which then leads to diabetes.

Adrenal gland disease (Cushing's)

Some cases of diabetes are linked to problems with the adrenal glands. When the adrenal glands become over-active they produce too much of a hormone called cortisol, which serves to elevate blood sugar. Cortisol also increases a cat's appetite and body weight, which are also risk factors leading to diabetes. This condition, where excess cortisol is produced, is called Cushings disease.

Chapter 3: What are the symptoms of diabetes?

By now you should have a good idea of what diabetes is and how it might come about. But would you know how to spot it in your cat? Here are some common symptoms to watch out for. Remember that only your vet can make an official diagnosis – there are lots of other conditions that can cause the symptoms below, and your vet needs to rule these out before coming to a diagnosis of diabetes.

Furthermore, the symptoms of diabetes usually develop very gradually and it might be a long time before you notice anything is wrong and report it to your vet. With diabetes, early diagnosis and treatment can avoid all sorts of serious complications. For this reason, it's vital to report any of the symptoms below as soon as they arise – don't wait and see if your cat recovers.

Steroid medications

If your cat has been taking steroid medication for an existing health condition such as a skin allergy, you should be aware that prolonged use of these steroids can affect the cat's delicate hormonal balance, causing high blood sugar. The good news is that some of these diabetes cases can be reversed, once the cat comes off the steroid medication.

Acromegaly

A disorder where the body produces too much growth hormone (acromegaly) can also be a cause of diabetes. This growth hormone, when produced in adults, can actually decrease the effectiveness of insulin. Usually this happens as a result of a tumour on the pituitary gland.

Pregnancy

Speaking of hormones, it's important to be aware that pregnancy can increase the risk of diabetes in your cat. Some cats, especially those in their older years and at the later stages in their pregnancies, can develop a sudden form of diabetes which tends to go away once the pregnancy is over. Again, the cause is hormonal – in this case it's thought to be caused by high levels of progesterone.

Urinating more frequently

Cats with diabetes need to eliminate all that excess glucose from their bodies, and they do so by urinating in large volumes. So, if you notice your cat starts to pee a lot more than usual, or maybe you're having to change his kitty litter a lot more frequently, it could be an indicator of diabetes. Of course, cats with urinary tract infections will also need to urinate frequently, but they will be straining and are usually in pain, whereas a cat with diabetes eliminates quite easily, and without discomfort. The reason he is peeing so often is that the excess glucose is drawing more water into the bloodstream through osmosis. The kidneys can't reabsorb this water because of its high glucose levels, so instead they filter the water out into the bladder.

Excessive thirst

Cats with diabetes are having to pee so often that they become constantly thirsty, to compensate for all the fluids they are losing through urinating. So if you are finding that you have to refill your cat's water bowl several times a day, it could be because of excessive thirst.

Weight loss

If a cat has had diabetes for a while, he is likely to be losing weight. This is because the body is no longer being provided with enough glucose as fuel. Instead of being able to use glucose to power metabolic processes, the body is forced to use fats and proteins. So, the cat's body fat will be decreasing bit by bit. It's a wise idea to weigh your cat regularly, even if he is completely healthy, so that you can easily spot this warning sign.

Over eating

Despite the fact that he is losing weight, your cat will probably show signs of overeating because his cells aren't getting the fuel they would normally get from glucose. So, to compensate for the lack of energy supply, he will have the urge to eat a lot more than usual. However, his body will be fighting an uphill struggle because without insulin, it can't make use of all of the glucose that it's being fed. The body is being forced to use its fat supplies instead – hence the continued weight loss.

Lethargy

Once your cat gets to the stage where he's losing weight as a result of diabetes, he will also become a lot less energetic and will be sleeping more. He might be reluctant to exercise, or simply less bouncy and animated than usual.

Symptoms of untreated diabetes

If diabetes is left untreated and unnoticed for a long time, you might also see some of the following symptoms in your cat, which are evidence of secondary medical conditions.

Bacterial Infections

Diabetic cats are much more prone to infections in the body, whether it's skin infections, gum infections or urinary tract infections. Cats in particular can have recurring issues with the urinary tract. This is because the high levels of sugar in the blood provide a breeding environment for bacteria. You can imagine how much discomfort a urinary infection can cause a cat who is already trying to eliminate excessive amounts of urine.

For this reason, if your cat has diabetes, he should have his urine tested on a regular basis. Gum disease is also a risk, because the tartar on teeth floods the bloodstream with bacteria, which breeds faster in a body that is full of glucose. Brush your cat's teeth very regularly, ideally every day, to combat this. If your otherwise healthy cat is having recurring infections in the mouth or urinary tract, you should have him tested for diabetes.

Fungal infections

Fungal infections are also an issue associated with diabetes. This is because the sugar in the blood actually feeds the fungus, leading to an infestation. Fungal or yeast infections can happen in the mouth, ears and reproductive organs.

Liver damage

Diabetes can put unnecessary strain on the liver. In particular, when the body can't gain access to glucose as a means of fuel, it will break down fat instead. This fat has to be broken down by the liver and if the liver is forced to process too much, it can accumulate and cause long term damage. This can be serious, and must be treated as soon as possible.

Cataracts

Cataracts are more commonly seen in diabetic dogs, but they can also be seen in cats in rare cases.

Toxicity (ketoacidosis)

When the cat's body is forced to break down fat for fuel instead of using glucose, the fat that is broken down releases ketones into the bloodstream. These ketones can build up to toxic levels, a condition called ketoacidosis in humans. When this happens, cats will feel very ill and will lose their appetites, with vomiting and diarrhoea. In this state, they will become very dehydrated and can even fall into a coma. If you suspect ketoacidosis, you must take your cat to the vet immediately. We will cover these "diabetic emergencies" in more detail later on in the book.

Chapter 4: How is diabetes diagnosed?

So, you've familiarised yourself with the common and not so common symptoms of diabetes. Now it's time to visit the vet for a diagnosis. Here is a useful breakdown of the ways your vet might test your cat for this condition. Remember that every cat is different, so what might prove conclusive for one cat might not necessarily be conclusive for yours – you have to trust your vet in these cases.

Older cats and cats with pre-existing medical conditions might take a little longer to examine because their symptoms can be caused by a variety of things besides diabetes. If you're not sure how the vet has come to his diagnosis, be sure to ask plenty of questions. The chances are, he will give a thorough explanation for his conclusions. If not, there is absolutely nothing to stop you from getting a second opinion elsewhere.

Your cat's medical history

The first thing the vet will want to do is have a quick chat with you about your cat's symptoms. You should mention everything you can think of at this stage, even if it seems like something small. Your vet might want to know things like how your cat is eating, drinking and eliminating. Lifestyle factors such as diet and obesity are also important to discuss. Finally, your vet might ask whether there is any history if diabetes in your cat's bloodline – although this is sometimes difficult to tell without speaking to your breeder.

Urine analysis

Once you've had a chat, and if the vet suspects diabetes, he will want to take a urine sample. This is quite straightforward and involves using a dipstick in a container of your cat's urine. This will test for the presence of glucose in your cat's pee, which is a major sign that there is diabetes. This is because the kidneys eliminate excess glucose via the urinary system, often because they have become overloaded with glucose they just can't cope with. The same sort of urine test will also show if your cat has a urinary infection. This could be one reason why your cat has been urinating excessively, or it could be a secondary effect of diabetes. So, urine tests are very useful when it comes to diagnosing diabetes.

Blood sugar test

Your vet will also look at the amount of glucose present in the blood, to see if it has reached abnormally high levels. However, this test alone is going to be inconclusive unless your vet can identify whether the high glucose levels have been that way for a while. This is because there are lots of factors, such as stress, which can temporarily raise your cat's blood sugar levels.

Blood chemistry profile

Besides testing your cat's blood for excess glucose, the vet might also want to do a blood chemistry profile to check all sorts of other things in your cat's blood, from hormone levels to electrolytes. Your vet knows what is normal and will be able to spot if something is out of kilter. It will also help determine whether the diabetes is severe, and if there have been certain complications as a result. For example, if there is a high level of ketones in your cat's blood, it may indicate ketosis, which is a potentially fatal condition that happens in untreated diabetes. Liver enzymes in your cat's blood can help the vet determine if there is liver disease. In addition, a blood count could help diagnose certain complications such as dehydration and blood cell rupture.

Fructosamine test

In addition to these tests, there is also something called a Fructosamine test. This test measures the amount of fructosamine in the blood, and is an indicator of the levels of glucose in the cat's blood over the past 2-3 weeks. Fructosamine is formed when glucose binds to proteins in your cat's bloodstream. So, when there is a high level of glucose in the blood, there will also be a high level of fructosamine and vice versa. These tests are useful when the cat's normal blood test shows only a slightly elevated glucose level, as they can confirm if the spike is temporary or something that has been going on for a while.

These are just some of the ways your vet will be able to detect diabetes. Be sure to ask your vet plenty of questions when you visit.

Chapter 5: Treating your cat's diabetes

Now that you've been to the vet and your cat has been diagnosed with diabetes, it's time to think about treatment going forward. Although diabetes sounds like a complex condition, the treatment is rather straightforward: in most cases, your cat is going to need regular insulin injections to help keep his blood sugar low. This chapter goes through the insulin side of things and explains the treatment for diabetes in more detail. Bear in mind that your cat will also need things like a nutritious diet (which we'll discuss later on), adequate exercise and treatment for any secondary issues that might arise. He will need a healthy, low stress lifestyle with an owner who is dedicated to his needs.

Insulin treatment

Insulin is a hormone that was discovered in 1921. The human form of diabetes had been known to medical professionals for a long time, but it wasn't until the discovery of insulin that diabetes went from a fatal condition to something that could be managed successfully. Many of the experiments that led to the discovery of insulin were performed on dogs, so we have our canine friends to thank for the fact that diabetes is no longer a death sentence for people and pets.

To give you an idea of where the insulin comes from that we treat our pets with, it is usually extracted from the pancreas of an animal such as a cow or a pig. Insulin can also be produced synthetically, thanks to advances in bio engineering that were made as early on as 1978, when insulin became the first human protein to be manufactured through biotechnology.

Finding the right insulin type and dosage

Insulin is usually given to cats in the form of daily injections. Sometimes, it can also be given as oral medication. The first thing to know about insulin treatment is that there are many, many insulin products out there which are used to treat diabetes in cats. Reactions to these products vary from cat to cat and not every product is designed to work in the same way. So, finding the right insulin type for your cat is often an ongoing process where you and your vet monitor your cat to see what works best.

Don't expect your cat's condition to improve overnight – it will take some time. Your vet may want to keep your cat in overnight to test his glucose levels over a 24 hour period. Or, he might want you to do that at home. With cats, it's often best that they are tested at home because the environment of the vet's clinic can be quite stressful, with lots of other animals, a strange environment, and different people coming and going. Stress can cause your cat's blood sugar to rise, so the results from an overnight stay might not be typical of a "normal" day for your cat. Speak to your vet if you're concerned about this.

Types of insulin

Insulin from pigs and humans are the closest types of insulin to that which is produced by cats, and therefore the safest.

The insulin your vet chooses for your cat will depend on factors like:
- How fast acting the insulin is (its “onset”)
- When the insulin works the hardest (its “peak time”)
- How long the insulin is effective for (its “duration”)

Why peak time, onset and duration are important

Insulin needs to be administered at exactly the right time (in relation to meal times) in order to work correctly. There needs to be enough sugars in the cat’s bloodstream at the time that the insulin takes effect for it to be able to perform its function. If there are no sugars in the cat’s bloodstream when the insulin takes effect, it will be of little or no use to the cat because there is no glucose there for the insulin to work on in the first place.

If the insulin has no glucose to act on, it will simply circulate in the cat’s body without bringing any benefits. If it is administered at the wrong time, it could also cause a hypoglycemic reaction (low blood sugar - one of the emergency situations we’ll discuss later on). So, timing is crucial.

Each cat will have a different daily routine and feeding times. Some cats are fed twice a day and some are fed once a day. Some cats have owners who are around all day and some are only home at certain times. This is why some insulin treatments have a long duration (staying active in the body for hours at a time) and some have a short duration. Just to give you some examples:

Short duration insulin acts in a very short space of time and will reach its peak activity quickly, before wearing off suddenly. A lot of the time, this type of insulin is used in emergency situations when a cat’s sugar level suddenly reaches high levels and needs to be stabilised quickly.

Intermediate acting insulin reaches its peak activity between 4 and 10 hours after it is first injected (this differs between brands). It delivers a steady amount of insulin activity for 16 hours after it is first injected. Many vets split this into two separate injections.

Long acting insulin starts to work within 6-10 hours and can stay active for up to 20 hours after it has been injected. This means it provides a more consistent level of insulin throughout the day.

The science behind insulin treatment might sound complex, but don't worry, your vet will do all the hard work and will work out what is best for your cat. All you have to do is be a diligent owner, and administer the insulin when you are told to, in the correct dose.

Does insulin always have to be injected?

A small number of cats can be treated with oral medication (called Glucosol or Glipizide) which helps to lower the blood sugar by stimulating the pancreas to produce insulin. This medication will work for cats with type II diabetes (when the cat isn't producing enough insulin). However, these cases are the minority. By all means, ask your vet about this but bear in mind that the majority of cats need more effective treatment – insulin injected directly into the bloodstream.

These oral medications can have a number of unpleasant side effects and aren't suitable for cats with existing liver or kidney disease. They can also lead to further pancreatic damage because they stimulate the pancreas to produce abnormal amounts of proteins. For this reason, they are generally only used as a last resort where it isn't possible to give the cat an injection.

Administering insulin

When exactly you give your cat insulin and, how often, is going to be up to your vet to decide. Don't try to change the schedule or dose without your vet's advice, or you could have a very sick cat on your hands! There are two possibilities: either your vet will want you to give the insulin once a day, or twice a day. In addition, most vets will suggest that you give your cat insulin just after his meal. This is because he won't need as much insulin if he eats less than usual. There is a risk of giving your cat hypoglycemia if he does not eat but is still given insulin.

What dose of insulin will my cat need?

Each cat is different, so please don't go by what you read on forums or what your friend who has a diabetic cat does. This is because:

- Some cats continue to make a small amount of insulin on their own
- Each cat stores and metabolises insulin in its own way
- Different brands and types of insulin affect cats in their own way

It may take several weeks for your vet to find the right dosage of insulin for your cat. In the meantime, be patient and be as proactive as you can about monitoring your cat's health.

Testing your cat's blood sugar and plotting a glucose curve

You will usually be asked to check your cat's blood glucose levels before meals and an hour after eating, as well as half way through the day (in the first few days of diagnosis you may need to do this hourly). To do this, you will need a glucometer, a hand held device which measures the amount of glucose in the blood. You can then plot a "glucose curve" (a basic line graph) which will show your cat's glucose levels and when they peak and drop during the day. Now that your cat is diabetic, your job will be to keep these glucose levels as steady as possible, rather than having lots of peaks and troughs.

To test your cat's blood sugar with the glucometer, you will need to collect a tiny drop of blood from your cat's ear, inner lip or elbow - wherever causes the least pain. The drop of blood then needs to be analysed by the glucometer. Ideally, the glucometer needs to be one that's made especially for cats and not one for humans because they have a different blood chemistry.

Don't worry – your cat will get quite used to having this done and if he is rewarded with a treat afterwards, he may even come to look forward to it! Once you know your cat's insulin curve, your vet will be able to devise a suitable schedule for administering the insulin.

Note that before you can prepare an accurate insulin curve, you will need to give your cat a few days for his body to get used to the insulin. The insulin curve will be more accurate if it's prepared at home, where the cat has a normal routine. In the animal hospital, your cat will be under all sorts of stress and the glucose readings won't be indicative of a normal day.

How to give insulin to your cat

Once your vet has given you instructions for your cat's insulin dose, it's time to master the art of injecting the treatment. There are a number of different methods for injecting cats with insulin, and different cats can respond well to different areas of the body.

Your vet will demonstrate the best way to do this, and you should take notes if possible. However, here is a general guide for you in the meantime.

1. Before you begin:

Take some time to warm up the insulin to room temperature, which will minimise the discomfort for your cat.

- It's best if you can incorporate the insulin injection within a set routine so that your cat comes to expect it. For example, feed your cat, let him wash himself afterwards and then take him in your lap for some grooming or petting. During this time, you can give the injection, and the cat will come to expect it and be calmer as a result.
- Don't try to take your cat off guard – cats hate to be surprised and will quickly realise something is up! They will respond much better if the injection is expected.
- Have a low carb treat ready to reward your cat after he has had the injection.

2. Filling the syringe

It's essential to use a syringe that's been made for your brand of insulin. This is so you can get the measurements right – giving slightly over or under the right amount can have a big effect on your cat's health.

If you aren't sure whether you have the right syringe, ask your vet to recommend a suitable one. Also, before you begin, check whether the area where you live has any laws on where you can and can't dispose of syringes. Hygiene is really important when it comes to these medical procedures, both for your cat and for the environment.

- Don't re-use a syringe– syringes can become damaged and it simply isn't hygienic for your cat.
- When you fill the syringe, do it very slowly and try to avoid creating any air bubbles. If there are any air bubbles in the syringe, you need to empty it back into the bottle and fill it up again.

3. Choosing where to give the injection

Some cat owners believe that the scruff of the neck is the best place to give a cat an injection, because there is less sensitivity there. Unfortunately, this is bad advice – the scruff of the neck (where the mother would usually pick up a kitten) has a poor blood supply so this will hinder the absorption of the insulin. So, try not to use that spot unless you absolutely have to.

Instead, choose a spot on the side of your cat's body, avoiding the sensitive area of the abdomen and nipples. It's important to choose a different place for the injection each time, because if the same spot is always used, it can be very painful and can also cause a knot of tissue called a granuloma which becomes cut off from the blood supply.

Giving the injection

Now it's time to give the injection. Make sure you're feeling calm and confident – your cat will pick up on your mood and may start to struggle otherwise. The first few times will be a bit tricky but you will get used to the process, becoming more and more confident as time goes on. Don't become so confident that you become complacent though! Giving insulin requires concentration, and you must take care to give exactly the right amount or you could make your cat very ill.

- Pinch some loose skin between your thumb and forefinger. If you have a long haired cat, you might find it easier to trim some of the fur so you can see whether you're injecting into the cat's skin or into the fur. Accidentally injecting into the fur is going to be no use whatsoever to your cat!
- At this stage, you might find it useful to do a few practice pinches of the skin, so that your cat is unaware of which pinch the injection will come in. However, if you inject properly, going under the skin rather than into the skin, and avoiding the muscle, then your cat shouldn't feel pain and will barely notice the needle going in. Use a firm pinch to help numb the area.
- Once you have pinched the skin, it's time to inject. You want the needle to go underneath the skin, not into the skin itself. Otherwise, the insulin isn't reaching the bloodstream properly. To do this, you need to hold the syringe almost parallel to your cat's spine, but at a slight angle so that the needle is pointing slightly downwards. Penetrate the skin quickly, smoothly and confidently and you will cause less pain. Once the needle is in, gently inject the insulin.
- After the injection you can praise your cat and give him a healthy treat to reward him.

What if the insulin doesn't seem to be working?

If the insulin you give your cat doesn't lower his blood sugar levels as expected, there are several avenues to investigate. Check the following:

- Are you storing the insulin correctly and is the bottle still within its use-by date?
- Are you giving the correct amount, and using the right syringe?
- Is your glucometer working properly? You may want to use a sec-

ond one and compare the results.

What factors can affect insulin?

If you can rule out all of the above, then your vet will probably either change your cat's dosage, or put him on a different type of insulin. However, it's important to bear in mind that the following factors can also affect how your cat responds to insulin:

- Being overweight, which makes it difficult for some cats to utilise insulin
- Cats that are taking corticosteroids for an existing health issue might seem resistant to insulin, because these medications cause blood sugar to rise
- If you have a female that isn't spayed, the high levels of progesterone during a heat can make the blood sugar rise and will make insulin less effective
- Pets that are anaemic or dehydrated may have a higher blood glucose reading than normal
- Sometimes giving a dose of insulin that's too large can have a rebound effect (known as the "Somogyi effect"), where the blood sugar drops rapidly but bounces back up again because the body suddenly produces lots of cortisol and adrenalin in response. This kind of rebound affect will show on a glucose curve, and is something to watch out for.

What to ask your vet about insulin

It can seem daunting for you and your cat when you first get a diabetes diagnosis. Stay calm and focus on gathering as much information as you can to help you in the coming weeks. Remember that finding the right balance of insulin is going to take some time.

Knowing what to do in an unusual situation (such as forgetting a dose) can be a huge help and will save you making emergency phone calls. So, take a pen and paper with you to the vet's and jot down the answers to the following useful questions:

- How important is it to give the insulin at a certain time of day?
- What should I do if I miss an insulin dose?
- How many hours or minutes late can I give the insulin dose?
- Should I adjust the dose if I'm giving insulin at a later time than usual and, if so by how much?
- If I gave the last insulin dose late, should the following injection be at the normal time?
- If my cat has refused to eat, should I still give him insulin?
- If my cat only eats a part of his meal, should I still give him the same amount of insulin?
- What should I do if my cat vomits his meal up, after I've given him insulin?
- What should I do if I find my cat has eaten a lot more than usual by accident? (i.e. he has been fed by someone else, or has been eating scraps he found)

Chapter 6: Danger signs in diabetic cats

There will be times when your cat's blood sugar isn't managed properly, or is affected by something you can't control, such as stress or a secondary medical condition. Cats are notorious for being finicky eaters, and this can also affect their blood sugar levels from day to day. In order to be well prepared for these situations, you need to familiarise yourself with the danger signs in diabetic cats. Here are the most important signs to be aware of.

Hypoglycemia

Hypoglycemia happens when a cat is given too much insulin and, as a result, their blood sugar drops to dangerously low levels.

This can happen if:

- The dose given was too large for their current needs
- The dose given was accidentally higher than usual

- The cat hasn't eaten, so it needs less insulin than usual
- The cat has exercised more than usual, meaning it needed less insulin than was given

In cats with hypoglycemia, the first signs you will notice are restlessness, disorientation or loss of coordination, shivering or trembling, and becoming unusually hungry. However, if the blood sugar stays low for longer and is left untreated, the symptoms will progress and the cat will become sleepy, lethargic, and will eventually lose consciousness. He may have seizures. It can very quickly become a serious condition.

In mild cases, the first thing you must do is try to feed your cat his normal food as soon as possible. Check your cat's blood glucose level with your glucometer and if the cat's levels are abnormally low, try to figure out what could have caused it. If the problem is serious and your cat is losing consciousness, you should take your cat to the vet immediately. If you aren't sure, you should make a call to your vet to see if you need to bring your cat for an examination.

If your cat is struggling to stay conscious there is very little chance of getting him to eat something. In addition, it could be dangerous to force a cat in this condition to eat as he could very easily choke. In these cases you need to have a source of liquid glucose readily available. Every owner of a diabetic cat should keep something for these emergency situations.

Here are some suggestions:

- Ask your vet to provide you with a suitable glucose solution for emergency situations
- Get some glucose tablets from your local pharmacy and dissolve them in water

In general, a cat that is hypoglycemic will need a certain amount of glucose per pound of body weight. Ask your vet for precise measurements. Some people give their cats things like sugary corn syrup, but this contains mostly fructose, which the body needs to convert into glucose. So, these foods are slower to act. It's best to make sure you have some kind of glucose in liquid form that is ready in your cupboard for these situations.

To give your cat glucose, the best thing to do is apply it to his lips and gums, or under the tongue. Be careful when doing this as some cats with hypoglycemia can be very disorientated and may try to bite. You can use a brush to apply the solution if you prefer.

The main thing is to act quickly, and give the glucose in small amounts at a time rather than in one big dose. Keep a close eye on your cat and as he recovers, let him eat something if he wants to.

Keep in mind that the glucose will only have a very short effect and will give your cat a sugar high that will quickly wear off. So, you may need to give him more after a short time. In general though, once he is well enough to eat then the carbohydrate in his diet will replenish his glucose levels just fine. Be sure to have a proper chat with your vet afterwards to see if you can pinpoint what caused the hypoglycemia to occur.

Severe dehydration

When a diabetic cat gets hypoglycemia, severe dehydration can result. Water is literally sucked out of the vital organs such as the brain by osmosis. Water will also be lost in huge amounts through urinating excessively. The cat will become very weak and lethargic, and will lose all interest in eating or drinking. Eyes will become sunken and the skin will lose all of its elasticity.

If things are left untreated the cat will fall into a coma and there is a slim chance of recovery. However, if caught in time, the cat can be put on an IV drip and have fluid replacement therapy, as well as having things like potassium replenished.

One thing to be aware of is that cats who eat a diet solely comprised of dry kibble will need a lot more water than those who eat wet, tinned food (yet another reason why most cat kibble is unsuitable for diabetic cats).

Ketosis

You might have heard the stories about the Atkins diet, where people starve themselves of carbohydrates in order to make their bodies use their fat reserves for fuel instead. This can make people feel very sick with headaches and bad breath, and the reason for this is that it puts them in a state of ketosis. With diabetic cats, the same can happen. This is because without insulin, they are starved of the glucose that the carbohydrates in their diets provide.

Their bodies are forced to metabolise fat instead, and when fat is broken down for fuel it produces ketones. Usually, there is always a small amount of ketones floating around in the bloodstream, but when these levels build up, they can cause a toxic level of acidity in the blood, making your cat very sick. This condition is known as ketoacidosis and has the following symptoms:

- Vomiting
- Diarrhoea
- Dehydration
- Weakness and lethargy
- Rapid, shallow breathing
- Bad breath with an odd chemical smell

The ketones are present in the urine when this happens, and the condition can be fatal if left untreated. Often, ketoacidosis is the first sign that a cat has diabetes. cats with the condition need to be seen by a vet immediately, who will administer a fast acting insulin and replenish lost fluids via an IV drip.

A good way to avoid ketoacidosis is to test your cat's urine regularly to monitor its ketone levels. You can buy testing kits from your local pharmacy, or ask your vet to provide you with one.

Somogyi effect

Cats are particularly prone to something called the Somogyi effect, which is a rebound in blood sugar to sometimes dangerous levels. This happens when the cat's blood sugar drops dangerously low (perhaps in response to an insulin dose that is too high for the cat to cope with). When the blood sugar drops too low, the liver pumps out glucose to compensate, which results in a sudden spike in glucose levels.

To an observer, this might look like the insulin simply hasn't worked. In reality, it has caused a rebound effect. On a glucose curve this will be visible as sudden peaks and troughs, although you are unlikely to be monitoring your cat at the exact time this is happening. Usually, if your cat's blood glucose is higher (rather than lower, as it should be) after an increased dose of insulin, then you should suspect the Somogyi effect.

High blood pressure

Diabetic cats have a higher risk of developing hypertension, or high blood pressure. This can lead to kidney damage over time. You should have your cat's blood pressure checked each time you visit the vet if possible.

Nerve damage

In rare cases diabetic cats can be prone to nerve damage, which usually presents itself as weakness in the hind legs. Cats with this condition appear to be walking on their hocks rather than their feet, which looks rather odd. If you spot anything like this in your cat, report it to your vet immediately.

Reactions with other medicines

If your cat is already on other medication, you need to be aware of any possible interference with insulin levels. Medications that affect the liver, muscle or fat tissue are especially risky, so always be sure to ask your vet if you have concerns. Corticosteroids, many of which are used to treat allergies, can interfere with the effectiveness of insulin. Antibiotics, diuretics, thyroid treatments and even aspirin can alter your cat's glucose levels so be sure to discuss these with your vet.

Chapter 7: Managing diabetes

Your cat may have been diagnosed with diabetes, but rest assured that there is a considerable amount of light at the end of the tunnel. Whilst there is no cure, the condition can be managed quite easily with the right care and medication. Your cat can live quite a long, happy life provided he is lucky enough to have an owner who is good at managing a diabetic cat. This section will go through some tips for owners who are managing their pets' diabetes.

A new set of responsibilities

It goes without saying that the relationship you have with your cat, and your lifestyle, are going to change slightly now that you are dealing with diabetes. However, these changes will be worth it once you see your cat regaining his health and enjoying life once more. Some of the things you will need to think about include:

- Deciding who is going to be the person to administer insulin in your family, and making sure everyone knows how to do it in case that person is unavailable
- Making sure there is always someone at home to administer insulin, at the time it is required
- Finding the right person to look after your diabetic cat if you go away for the weekend, are on holiday or you need to visit family at the last minute
- Having emergency phone numbers in place if there are any complications
- Being prepared to give a more nutritious diet, and a careful regime of exercise in order to keep your cat in good health

What you will need

Now that you have a diabetic cat, you need to prepare yourself for the various risks and emergencies that can occur from time to time.

Here is a basic list of things you will need in your diabetes kit:

- Insulin
- Syringes
- Glucose solution for hypoglycemic emergencies (when blood sugar drops to dangerously low levels)
- A medical alert tag for your cat's collar (to tell people that your cat has diabetes)
- Glucometer (a hand held device for testing blood sugar)
- Glucose test strips
- Ketone test strips
- Air tight, sterile containers for storing syringes
- A small cooler bag for transporting insulin
- Spare bottle of insulin
- Emergency phone numbers for your vet
- A responsible, experienced pet sitter

You and your vet

If you are about to take on the task of managing your cat's diabetes, you need to build a solid relationship with your vet. If that means changing vets, then so be it. Your vet is going to need to be someone you trust, and someone who takes the time to explain the complexities of diabetes in simple, easy to understand language. The vet you decide to use should ideally possess the following qualities:

- Is situated close to your neighbourhood, so that if any emergencies occur you are within easy reach of the clinic
- Has great communication skills and interpersonal skills, and is never dismissive of your concerns
- Doesn't rush through examinations because they are too concerned about a queue of people in the waiting room
- Is compassionate and friendly with your cat, rather than detached or preoccupied
- Knows a lot about managing diabetes and has experience of helping owners manage the condition

To find a good quality vet, you might want to ask other cat owners if there is someone they recommend. You could also ask at your local pet shelter, or the breeder you got your cat from. Once you have a few recommendations your best bet, if possible, is to pay them each a visit before making a final decision.

Learning about treatment

Once you have had your cat diagnosed as diabetic, be sure to ask as many questions as you need to. Don't go home wondering why you've been told to do a certain thing for your cat, or why you aren't allowed to feed them a certain food. Try to gather as much information as you need. Ask if there is a number you can call if you have questions in the first few weeks, because it may take you some time to get used to managing the diabetes. Here are some examples of questions you may need to ask:

- How will the treatment (usually insulin) interact with other medications my cat is taking? How will it affect the health conditions my cat already has?
- What complications should I watch out for?
- What do I need to keep a record of in order to manage the diabetes properly?
- Why has the vet chosen that particular type or brand of insulin? If that type doesn't seem to be working, how long before they will try something else?
- How often does your cat need to have check-ups at the vet?
- How much is the treatment going to cost? How much will the check-ups be?

Remember that in the first few weeks of being diagnosed, your cat might need to have his progress monitored by the vet once every 1-2 weeks. So you will be seeing lots of each other! After a few months, once the dosage and type of insulin is correct, the need for check-ups will be less frequent.

Using responsible sources

One thing to be aware of when you're researching diabetes is that there will be a huge amount of information out there which vets can't police. There are cat owners on forums claiming that certain products worked wonders for their cats. That may be the case, but you have no way of knowing who these people are and whether their opinions can be trusted. Likewise with natural medicine and holistic treatments – there are a lot of people out there looking to make a quick buck from worried pet owners, knowing that a lot of people will try anything to make their cats feel better. Don't be fooled.

The only opinion you can really trust is your vet's – he is the only person who has examined your cat in person and has the expertise to make informed decisions. Books like the one you're reading are fine for background information, but they should never be a substitute for visiting your vet and having a proper chat with him about your cat's health. You owe it to your cat to be responsible when it comes to these matters.

Learning to cope as a caregiver

As the owner of a pet with diabetes, you might find certain coping mechanisms more useful than others. For example, you might start to blame yourself for your cat's diabetes, and wonder if it was something you did that caused him to develop the condition. This isn't helpful – there are so many factors that contribute to diabetes, and so much we still don't know about genetics, environment, diet and even biology. Ruminating about this stuff isn't going to bring your cat back to perfect health.

In reality, the only thing that will help your cat to cope with diabetes is having an owner who is happy and healthy enough to be the best possible carer. That means keeping your stress levels low, learning to look after your own needs as well as your cat's, and knowing when to ask for support from friends, family members and your vet. Remember that this condition can be managed and there are thousands of cat owners around the world doing it quite successfully. So don't lose heart! Why not set up a support group for owners of diabetic cats in your area? Or participate in online discussions with people who understand what you're dealing with?

Chapter 8: Feeding and exercising dogs with diabetes

Besides treating your cat with insulin, you are going to have to make a few important lifestyle changes. The most important of these changes will be diet and exercise. Here are some important changes you will need to make in these areas.

How important is diet in treating diabetes?

Most vets agree that diet is extremely important, not only to support the diabetes but to keep the cat as healthy as possible so that complications don't arise. Coping with diabetes is already a challenge, without having to deal with secondary health conditions, so do yourself and your cat a favour and keep your cat in excellent shape with the right diet and plenty of exercise. In addition, some cats with very mild diabetes can go into remission once their diets have been improved.

Here are some important facts:

- Fatty diets, and being obese can interfere with the effectiveness of insulin
- Diets that are high in carbohydrates are very bad for diabetic cats
- A diet that's low in carbohydrates, high in protein with a small amount of fat can help to keep diabetes under control

With these facts in mind, here are some qualities to look for in your cat's food:

Low fat

Avoid feeding your cat any foods which contain high levels of grease and fat. This can make insulin less effective once administered and it can also lead to weight gain and further health issues. Don't be fooled by dry kibble foods – these have often been sprayed with grease to make them more palatable and to disguise some of the less tasty ingredients. The grease is often oxidised and this puts more stress on the digestive system.

Low carbohydrate and low sugar

Avoid any foods with lots of simple sugars, or carbohydrates. Cats generally don't need carbohydrates as a rule, and by feeding them to your cat you will only be contributing to an already high blood sugar, thus worsening the symptoms of diabetes. One of the main reasons commercial cat foods contain carbs is simply because they bulk out the food and are a cheap ingredient. There is not really any nutritional value for your cat, since cats are natural carnivores and their ancestors ate a diet purely made up of animal fat and protein.

Avoid fish products

A lot of cat foods that contain fish products are produced with very poor quality fish (usually the parts that are not suitable for human consumption). The fish is usually rancid before it gets to the factory, and is treated with all sorts of chemicals and preservatives as a result. These ingredients can act as toxins and may produce an inflammation in your cat's pancreas, which is guaranteed to make diabetes worse. So, they are best avoided.

Choose treats wisely, and give them sparingly

Treats are very useful for any cat owner because they act as a reward system for training and soothing. For diabetic cats, treats need to be kept to a minimum because they can lead to weight gain and unwanted spikes in blood sugar. So, choose your treats carefully. Make sure they have a low calorie count, and are low in fat. Natural, rather than processed treats are a good idea – lean cuts of cooked meat, for example.

Avoid "semi moist" foods

There are some cat foods on the market that, rather than being wet, tinned food, are advertised as "semi moist". Avoid these foods as they contain some nasty preservatives and artificial ingredients which will only harm your cat. Lots of them contain dextrose, fructose and glycerin which are harmful to cats with diabetes.

Feed a high quality cat food

When it comes to keeping a diabetic cat healthy, one of the best things you can do is to choose a high quality, nutritious food for your cat. This will keep him trim and healthy. Avoid the cheap, supermarket brands of cat food as they often contain unnecessary "filler" ingredients with no nutritional value.

Feeding schedules and diabetes

Because food is the main way your cat gets his glucose, you need to be extra careful about your feeding regimen with a diabetic cat. Feed your cat the same amount every day, at the same time every day, and you will avoid complications which arise from mis-timing your cat's insulin shots. In addition to this, it's always better to feed your cat several smaller meals a day rather than one large meal, as this will help to keep blood sugar levels at an even keel, making sure they don't drop too low if the cat goes too long without food.

Conflicting opinions and research

There will be a lot of conflicting information on the subject of fibre for diabetic cats, so keep this in mind if you decide to research the topic. Remember that different cats will respond differently to fibre, and this will also depend on the cat's weight, age, breed and size. Keep in mind that there is no standard recommended diet for every diabetic cat – your vet will need to weigh up all the factors and give you an accurate idea of the ideal diet for your cat.

What to do if your cat is obese

If your diabetic cat is overweight then it's in his best interests to try and get his weight down gradually and safely, without resorting to crash diets. You can do this simply by gradually reducing the cat's calorie intake each day. Once he has lost weight, you should find your cat's diabetes is less severe because his cells will be more able to utilise the insulin. Speak to your vet about safely reducing your cat's portion size if he is overweight – it will have an effect on the amount of insulin you need to give him.

What to do if your cat is too thin

Being underweight is a common symptom of diabetes in cats. If your cat is underweight, be careful not to feed a cat food that's too high in fibre as anything that could interfere with his ability to metabolise food can be dangerous.

What about exercise?

In general, cats with diabetes need the same amount of exercise as cats without diabetes. The only difference is that the exercise itself needs to be regular. Your cat should ideally get the same level of exercise each day too. If a cat gets too much exercise in one day, he will need much less insulin than usual. Failing to recognise this could result in you administering too much insulin and this could result in hyperglycemia. So, you need to monitor your cat's exercise levels carefully. If, for example, he is allowed outside and he meets a feline friend and they do a lot of running and chasing each other, then you may need to adjust the insulin levels of his next shot.

Ask your vet if you're unsure how to proceed. For now, you need to be aware of the following:

- Exercise uses up the glucose in the blood, as the body uses up more of it for energy to fuel the muscles and heart
- Exercise speeds up the heart rate, circulation and metabolism which dramatically increases the rate at which insulin is absorbed
- Exercise leads to a much lower level of blood sugar or glucose

In case of emergencies, it's important to bring a source of glucose with you if you're taking your cat on a journey of any kind. This will help to revive him in case his glucose levels drop dangerously low, which may result in hypoglycemia.

Outdoor cats versus indoor cats

The subject of outdoor cats is one that is heavily debated amongst cat owners. Some owners argue that a cat that stays indoors all day is likely to become depressed and overweight. Others argue that a cat that is allowed outside is at risk of far too many dangers.

Now that your cat has diabetes, you need to put these arguments aside and realise the following:

- Your cat needs to be present for feeding times at the same time every day, in order for him to get his insulin at the right time
- Your cat's diet needs to be monitored carefully to avoid complications like hypoglycaemia, dehydration and ketosis
- If your cat gets more exercise than usual one day, you will need to know about it in order to adjust his insulin

Unfortunately, in light of the above, the likelihood of you being able to keep on top of your cat's condition whilst he is allowed to roam outdoors all day is slim. You run the risk of your cat getting into trouble with low blood sugar when you are not there to help. You also can't be sure how much exercise he is getting, whether he is eating extra food when out and about, or whether he is going to be at home during feeding times.

If you have an outdoor cat and you're worried that keeping him indoors is going to be too stressful, speak to your vet. The outdoor lifestyle is not completely off limits, but it isn't a wise idea. You could also consider building a cat run for him in your garden, or taking him outside on a leash for a while every day. Remember that indoor cats need to be encouraged to exercise, or they can become obese, which is bad news for diabetes.

Chapter 9: Diabetes FAQs

Diabetes is a complex condition and is a subject that could be covered by several books. It's highly likely that you still have several questions for your vet. Here are some of the most frequently asked questions that vets receive, and some useful answers.

Why are cats with diabetes more difficult to manage than other animals?

Cats are a little bit different to dogs and humans. For one thing, their small size means that they need a very small, precise measurement of insulin which can be easily misjudged if an owner doesn't concentrate. Cats are also more prone to stress and that can have an immediate effect on their blood sugar levels. They are also fussy eaters, so it can be difficult to monitor what they eat and this can change from day to day, making a set dose very problematic. With that said, you shouldn't be deterred from taking on the task of managing your cat's condition – with the support of your vet and regular check-ups you should be fine.

Is it true that some cats with diabetes can go into remission?

Yes. Because most cats have type II diabetes, where they haven't completely stopped producing insulin, there is a chance that a cat will make a recovery from diabetes once he has had treatment for a certain period.

In some cases, diet has a big part to play, especially if the cat has been fed a poor diet up till diagnosis and is then changed to a low carb diet instead. Likewise, if the diabetes has been the result of a certain medication, and the cat is taken off that medication, then the condition can be reversed. We don't know very much about why exactly cats go into remission, but we know that it's possible.

How long can my cat live with diabetes?

With modern veterinary science, the days of diabetes being a death sentence are thankfully over. With proper management and careful treatment, a diabetic cat can live for as long as a non-diabetic cat, provided no complications arise.

What should I do if my cat goes off his food and won't eat?

Apart from raising an alarm that something is wrong with your cat, a sudden loss of appetite has a knock-on effect in terms of glucose levels and insulin needs. If your cat has refused to eat and he misses a meal as a result, you will need to lower the amount of insulin you give him. Ideally, you will have asked your vet about this in advance and you will have a recommended dose for these situations written down somewhere.

If not, don't panic. Remember that giving a low amount of insulin for just one day is going to be far less harmful for your cat than giving an amount that's too high (which would result in hypoglycemia, or dangerously low blood sugar). If your cat misses more than one meal, he needs to visit the vet. A loss of appetite is one of the first indicators of illness in cats, so he will need a check-up.

Why can't I test my cat's urine for sugar, instead of his blood?

It would be much easier if you could simply rely on a urine test and a dip stick to tell you how high your cat's blood sugar is. Unfortunately, these tests aren't accurate enough to be relied on because they only measure the sugar that has leaked into the urine, and not the sugar in the blood. These are two different factors.

One reason for this is that the results shown in urine can be delayed from those present in the blood. Testing the blood is an instant indicator of your cat's glucose levels, and as we've seen, timing is everything when it comes to treating diabetes. Using a glucometer is much more accurate than a dipstick, although you should keep some dipsticks or paper trips handy to measure your cat's ketone levels if needed.

My cat's blood sugar seems to be higher, rather than lower, after his insulin injection. Why is this?

Your cat could be suffering from a rebound effect where the body produces glucose in response to a low blood sugar. This is obviously a cause for concern, and your cat will need to have his insulin dose adjusted. Refer to the chapter on danger signs for more information.

Should I have my cat spayed now that she has diabetes?

Because heat cycles can affect blood sugar, you might find that your cat's diabetes will be easier to manage once she has been spayed. Speak to your vet if you'd like to consider this for your cat.

Chapter 10: Glossary of terms for dog owners

Diabetes is a condition that's difficult to discuss without resorting to medical terminology, so in this book we've tried to leave out the more complex terms. However, you might find this glossary of diabetic terms a useful resource when it comes to researching your cat's condition.

Acidosis

A condition where there is too much acid in the blood, usually caused by a build-up of ketones (produced when diabetics burn fat instead of glucose)

Adrenal glands

Two glands located on top of the kidneys. These glands make stress hormones which affect the body's metabolism of carbohydrates.

Antibodies

Proteins that the body produces in order to attack foreign bodies such as bacteria. When the wrong type of insulin is used on dogs, it can produce an antibody reaction

Beta cells

These cells are located in the pancreas, in an area called the islets of Langerhan. They produce insulin which controls the level of glucose in the blood.

Carbohydrate

One source of energy that comes from your dog's food, in the form of sugars and starches that are broken down to form glucose.

Dextrose

A type of glucose that's derived from starches, and is used quite a lot in processed foods like syrups

Euglycaemia or Normoglycaemia

These terms describe the state of having a normal blood glucose concentration

Fructose

A kind of sugar that is found in fruits, vegetables, honey and artificially sweetened foods. Fructose isn't recommended for diabetics as it can have a negative effect on blood sugar.

Glycemic Control

The phrase used to describe the act of controlling the levels of glucose in the bloodstream

Hyperglycaemia

A condition where the levels of glucose in the blood (the blood sugar) are too high

Hypoglycaemia

A dangerous condition where the level of glucose in the blood falls dangerously low. Symptoms include weakness, trembling, vomiting and falling unconscious

Hepatic
When something is "hepatic" it means it relates to the liver, one of the organs affected by diabetes

Polydipsia
This is the medical term for excessive thirst, one of the major signs of diabetes in dogs

Polyphagia
This is the medical term for excessive eating or an abnormally high appetite, another common symptom of diabetes

Polyuria
This is the medical term for excessive urination, which happens a lot in untreated diabetes

Post-Prandial
This term describes something that happens after food is given to your dog

Renal
Anything "renal" relates to something happening in the kidneys

Renal Threshold
The amount of sugar the kidneys can handle before the sugar begins to spill over into the urine

Conclusion

Diabetes doesn't have to be a source of stress if you manage it efficiently and are careful with your cat's daily routine. Speak to any owner of a diabetic cat and they will tell you the same thing – all of the work involved in caring for a cat with diabetes is worth it to have a happy, healthy cat.

Now that you know more about diabetes and how it can affect your cat, you should be feeling more at ease with your cat's diagnosis. The road ahead is going to be challenging, but it will get easier. As the weeks go by you'll get more and more familiar with the daily routine of checking your cat's blood sugar and administering insulin – and remember, your vet will always be there to help if you need it.

We hope you've found this book useful and that you will keep it to refer back to whenever you need it throughout your cat's life. We wish you and your cat the very best.

Want to know more about looking after your pet?

The writer of this book, Dr. Gordon Roberts, is a veterinarian and owns a total of eight animal hospitals around the UK. He believes that the key to a healthy, happy pet is preventative care, which is only possible when pet owners take the initiative to educate themselves about their animals. As a result, Gordon has written dozens of useful reports on pet care in order to share his years of experience with discerning pet owners. As a thank you for purchasing this book, you can browse and download his specialist reports completely free of charge! You'll learn all sorts of useful information about how to spot possible health conditions early on, and how to make preventative care for your pet a priority, helping you save time and money on visits to the vet later on. To view and download these bonus reports, simply visit Gordon's website at: http://drgordonroberts.com/freereportsdownload/.

Best wishes,
Gordon

Printed in Great Britain
by Amazon